There is no greater tragedy than the death of a mother's child. The excruciating loss leaves most not only bereft, but speechless. This is why the elegy is poetry's highest and noblest calling, for it both articulates the heart's anguish while also illuminating the immutable and infrangible bond of love. Such art is made at no small cost: the bereaved poet endures to bear witness.

—Richard Jones, author of *The Correct Spelling & Exact Meaning*

These heartbreaking poems about the death of Alexis Rhone Fancher's son Joshua join a select group of books unique in their artistry and compelling in their soulful lament—Stan Rice's *Some Lamb*, which chronicles his daughter's death from leukemia, Richard Jones' poems on the drowning of his nephew Andrew, and Shelly Wagner's book *The Andrew Poems*. Fancher's poems are both painful to read and balm for the soul. The journey may be difficult, but the poems touch us with their heart's cry. A magnificent testament to the resilience of the human spirit.

—Jack Grapes, author of *The Naked Eye* and *All the Sad Angels*

The ache of the heart is fierce with loss, and Alexis Rhone Fancher reminds us that the indelible bond a mother has for her child is boundless: "no place is big enough to hold it." This poet shows, with breath-taking clarity and raw vision, the mortal hurt of a devastating loss—the loss of a child is the deepest cavity of sorrow: "…[I]t's nothing personal. / He died young." Fancher is a gifted woman, mother, poet, warrior. Her prayer-like dirges, sorrowful but so full of life and cadence, are stained-glass windows through which we can see the tendering of language to heal us. Fancher's heart is large, refuses to shut down to sorrow and loss, but instead, allows her brave and resilient voice to shine the light, to move us all forward into a state of grace. This is the ultimate tribute to her beloved son. You will come back to these poems again and again, for their stunning precision and affirmation—a most soulful testimony to love and life, "a kind of music played / on my bones."

—Cynthia Atkins, author of *In the Event of Full Disclosure*

Alexis Rhone Fancher's poetry, well-known for erotic candor, reveals in this new collection the agony of emotional intensity, the loss of joy after the death of a loved child. Her words dare you to turn the page; there is no choice and no escape. Her words do not waver.

—Peter Neil Carroll, author of *Fracking Dakota: Poems for a Wounded Land*

Alexis Rhone Fancher's book, *State of Grace: The Joshua Elegies*, maps in searing detail a landscape no parent ever wants to visit—a mother's world after it's flattened by her child's death. Though her son's early passing was "nothing personal," her poems howl with personal devastation. They insist that the reader take the seat next to hers in grief's sitting room and "imagine him in his wooden forever." Fancher grapples with how to reconcile oneself to the slow loss of memory's fade-out, and with how to go on living without betraying the dead, how to "[s]queeze the life out of / her life." You'll need tissues when you read this book, but it's well worth rubbing your heart raw against the beauty of these poems and their brave, fierce honesty.

—Francesca Bell, eight-time nominee for the Pushcart Prize in poetry, and winner of the 2014 Neil Postman Award for Metaphor from *Rattle*

Tender and tough, plainspoken and eloquent, Alexis Rhone Fancher's elegies for her son are marvels of insight, honesty, and feeling. Abandon hope, advised Dante, as his seeker entered the kingdom of death. And in Fancher's inferno, hope is in short supply. What we have instead are anger, pleading, and denial. "I should have saved him. That's what mothers do," she declares, in thrall to her impossible wish. Her grief haunts her like her memories of her son. Only at the end of the sequence does she find some solace, the work of the imagination, the work of poetry filling her like a vision of the pregnant moon, "with her big belly, complicit, out in the darkness, lighting the way."

—Lee Rossi, author of *Wheelchair Samurai*

State of Grace:

The Joshua Elegies

by

Alexis Rhone Fancher

State of Grace: The Joshua Elegies
By Alexis Rhone Fancher

ISBN: 978-0-98-627032-1

First edition: 2015

Published by KYSO Flash Press: www.kysoflash.com

Book was designed and formatted by Clare MacQueen, in
collaboration with Alexis Rhone Fancher.

Poems are reprinted from several journals and magazines. Please
see Acknowledgments for details.

Please send questions and comments to:

Author: alexis@lapoetrix.com

Publisher: KYSOWebmaster@gmail.com

Also by Alexis Rhone Fancher:

How I Lost My Virginity to Michael Cohen:
and other heart-stab poems

Dedicated to Joshua Dorian Rhone
and Riley Thomas Brenner

Table of Contents

Foreword

Alexis Rhone Fancher didn't choose to write these poems. She would rather have written about something else. But she was compelled to write them by her unflinching love for her son, and I am grateful she did.

When I met Alexis in 2011, I was struck by her strength, compassion, and grace. She was four years ahead of me in the grieving process for her son Josh, dead at twenty-six, than I was for my son, Riley, who had recently died at the age of six. She inspired and empowered me. She showed me what it could look like to survive the death of a child four years later. It gave me hope.

Alexis's essence bleeds into these poems. There are the vivid, sensuous images that she is known for: "…its fresh linen smell and deep sinking…" and "…her long shadow spilling into the street," from "Dying Young." Everything slows down when I'm reading her poems. It feels like I'm in the room with her.

I appreciate her brutal honesty and surprising dialogue in "Over It" and "Death Warrant," two of my favorite poems in the collection. I am left haunted by lines from "Snow Globe," like this one: "Unless I look in the mirror I can't see him."

Alexis has created a stunning and unwavering collection of poems that takes grief head on. I don't know if writing them was healing for her, but I do believe that sharing her poems will help heal others.

This is a work of art filled with pain, love, and so much beauty it cannot be contained.

—Chanel Brenner
(Author of *Vanilla Milk*)
August, 2015

Author's Note:

The Supermarket
and a State of Grace

The supermarket is a good place to grieve. I can roam from aisle to aisle, safe behind dark glasses. I can cry unnoticed. When this ritual first began, a man came up to me and asked if I was all right. I must have cried out, sobbed loud enough to be heard. That was before I learned to weep silently. I'm better at it now. I've had practice.

I like the produce aisles. I like comparing golden beets to red ones, romaine to butter lettuce, and reading the recipes they put up next to the more exotic fruits and vegetables, so you'll know how to cook them. I enjoy planning meals in my head. It seems to take some of the pressure off. Tonight I'll make a crab and mango salad with champagne vinaigrette, Tom Yum Gai (except I'll use fish stock and shrimp instead of chicken) and grilled Asian salmon over skinny asparagus for the main course. I like keeping whole shopping lists in my head. It makes it too crowded to think.

But sometimes my supermarket strategy doesn't work. The experts say you must take the time to grieve, and grieve for "as long as it takes," but the opening isn't always there. A friend sent me something called "Mourner's Rights" but the title depressed me too much to read it. Ditto for that devastating book two different people sent to me, entitled *Who Dies?* meaning which part of a human being dies—ceases to exist—and what remains. Would that be the spirit? The soul? And if it remains, *where* does it remain? And how can the living access it? I didn't read that far.

If I knew how to access the spirit, maybe I could rest. Or maybe the spirit is the process, and I'm too overwhelmed to see. Or it could be that I can't access it because it's not possible, or maybe I'm plain not worthy. But I would give anything to know that he's okay. That he is whole and safe. That he is aware of my great love for him and my devastation at not being able to save him. I should have saved him. That's what mothers do.

I've made subtle life adjustments. I use only waterproof mascara. I walk the high wire of the produce aisle, avoid the mausoleum of the store's processed middle. And I never cry while shopping with other people; I suck it up. Mothers are supposed to do that, too. The sharing of my sorrow does nothing but spread it around.

I don't know how to deal with my son's dying when he was twenty-six, other than just to deal with it. Do what I'm doing and try not to collapse everything in my life into grief while still grieving. It's a bit of an Elvira Madigan, a tightrope walk I like to call Grace. Something to aspire to. As long as I stay on the tightrope, one foot in front of the other, arms held out to balance, I'm in a State of Grace, which is the space between the tightrope and the ground. It's peaceful there and my mind stops making everything mean something; as if knowing the meaning would make any difference.

—Alexis Rhone Fancher
January, 2008

Acknowledgments

"The Competition" is dedicated to Cliff Eisner.
"Dying Young" is dedicated to Kate O'Donnell.

Several poems in this collection were first published in the following magazines and journals:

Blotterature, Ekphrastic Edition:
"when her son is dead seven years" *

Broad!:
"Dying Young"
"Death Warrant"

Deep Water Literary Journal:
"The Lost Child"

KYSO Flash:
"My Dead Boy's Right Arm"
"The Competition" *

Rattle:
"Over It"

The MacGuffin:
"Mahogany Funeral Urn"
"Snow Globe"

* Nominated for the 2015 Best of the Net Awards and Anthology

Thank you, Chanel Brenner, for your brilliance, talent, friendship, and always open heart.

Thanks to Michelle Bitting for editing the early poems, and to Tim Green and Gordon Krupsky for publishing them.

Thank you, Elaine Amromin, Noelle Babakhyi, Amy Bisogni, Kevin and Jason Brody, Jason and Melissa Estevez, Lynol Gaskin, Jack Grapes, Bambi Here, Tony Magistrale, Kate O'Donnell, and Oliver Wishni for your love and support.

Thanks to my fierce editor, Tresha Faye Haefner, for holding my feet to the fire. Thanks to Clare MacQueen for publishing and believing in this chapbook.

And to my beloved Fancher: I could never have survived this without you.

Dying Young

Midnight, and again I'm chasing
sleep: its fresh-linen smell and
deep sinking, but when I close my eyes I see
my son, closing his eyes. I'm afraid of that dream,
the tape-looped demise as cancer claims him.

My artist friend cancels her L.A. trip. Unplugs the
internet. Reverts to source. If cancer
will not let go its grip, then she will
return its embrace. Squeeze the life out of
her life. Ride it for all it's worth.

By the time his friends arrive at the cabin
my son is exhausted, stays behind while
the others set out on a hike. He picks up the phone.
"Mom, it's so quiet here. The air has never
been breathed before. It's snowing."

I put on Mozart. A warm robe. Make a pot
of camomile tea. The view from my 8th floor
window, spectacular, the sliver moon, the stark,
neon-smeared buildings, their windows dark.
Sometimes I think I am the only one not sleeping.

My artist friend wants to draw the rain. She
wants to paint her memories, wrap the canvas
around her like a burial shroud.

Tonight, a girl in a yellow dress stands below
my window, top lit by a street lamp, her long shadow
spilling into the street. She's waiting for someone.

I want to tell my friend I'll miss her.
I want to tell my son I understand.
I want to tell the girl he won't be coming.
That it's nothing personal. He died young.

Death Warrant

When my son's ticket was about
to go to warrant, I went to the
courthouse and explained to the judge
that he was in the hospital, dying.
Someone gasped.
Someone grabbed my hand.

Josh lusted over a muscle car, a
Dodge Charger with a Hemi-powered,
5.7L V8 under the hood.
He wanted me to buy it. I wanted to
lease it. He said that meant I
knew he was going to die.

The judge looked over the warrant.
"He's in the hospital, you say?"
"Yes, your Honor. Terminal cancer."
"Good," she said. She handed the
paperwork back to the bailiff.
"Then he won't be driving
without a license,
out there endangering others."

The Competition

Thank you for coming.

After I put my despair on display,
and read those poems about
my dead son, I'm cornered by a stranger

who tells me he was orphaned
at sixteen. His mom was driving. He
walked away from the crash.

He tells me there's a name for what
we survivors bear. Traumatic Grief.
A recognized condition. PTSD for the bereaved.

I could one-up him; my mom's
early death, or the asleep-at-the-wheel
trucker who killed my boyfriend and our
baby when I was nineteen,

make it a competition
I know I'd win.
Instead, I default, tell him *I'm so sorry.*

When he hugs me I'm swallowed
by the weight of our common loss. I want
him to take it all away.

Instead, when I go home, I carry twice what
I had before. PTSD. Survivor's Guilt.
Our despair, and its proper name.

Baby Boy Blues

When he was born,
the old ladies peered
into the cradle,
cooed and clucked.

"If he lives," one of
them whispered,
"he'll be a real looker."

Snow Globe

Despair arrived, disguised as
nine pounds of ashes in a
velvet bag, worried so
often between my fingers
that wear-marks now stain
the fabric.

Is it wrong to sift
the remains of my dead son,
bring my ashen finger to my
forehead, make the mark of
the penitent above my eyes?

His eyes, the brown of mine,
the smooth of his skin, like mine.
Unless I look in the mirror
I can't see him.

Better he'd arrived
as a snow globe, a small figure,
standing alone at the bottom of his
cut-short beauty.

Give him a shake, and watch
his life float by.

Denial

I'm working on how
to text the dead. Fourth wall down.
My life not broken.

Mahogany Funeral Urn

My son was only twenty-six, and I couldn't bear the
thought of him six feet under ground, his death
a crappy movie I was forced to sit through,
flash forward through the rough spots, slo-mo
the sweet. Wishing I could rewind. Recast the lead.
Make him stick around. As if he had a choice.

I imagine him in his wooden forever, his ashes
gathered in a thoughtful fleece bag from the mortuary.
I remember the shock on her face when I told the
funeral arranger I wanted to take him To Go, that
I would place him on a shelf, beside his Jordan's,
his posters, his basketball, his impeccable wardrobe,
his hip-hop CDs, the snapshot of his beautiful
girlfriend, and yes, his despair, when he knew
this game, he would lose.

Out there, these traces of him. A voicemail. A text.
The night, a shining star. Each day, no mercy,
fresh grief. No place big enough to hold it.
Mark, my friend, is cutting a funeral urn out of
mahogany. He called and asked how big it should be.
"Big enough to hold it all."

The Lost Child

Mother's Day—it's the
Hallmark equivalent of
arrows in my heart.

Over It

Now the splinter-sized dagger that jabs at my heart has
lodged itself in my aorta, I can't worry it
anymore. I liked the pain, the
dig of remembering, the way, if I
moved the dagger just so, I could
see his face, jiggle the hilt and hear his voice
clearly, a kind of music played on my bones
and memory, complete with the hip-hop beat
of his defunct heart. Now what am I
supposed to do? I am dis-
inclined toward rehab. Prefer the steady
jab jab jab that reminds me I'm still
living. Two weeks after he died,
a friend asked if I was "over it."
As if my son's death was something to get
through, like the flu. Now it's past
the five-year slot. Maybe I'm okay that he isn't anymore,
maybe not. These days,
I am an open wound. Cry easily.
Need an arm to lean on. You know what I want?
I want to ask my friend how her only daughter
is doing. And for one moment, I want her to tell me she's
dead so I can ask my friend if she's over it yet.
I really want to know.

Never Forget Why Your Wrist Throbs

Look, when the insurance runs out,
the ulna sets itself

that clutch-at-the-railing/tumble down
two flights of Victorian stairs,
babe in arms, your wrist

eagerly sacrificed to save him.

Twenty-some years later,
after the boy gets cancer
and dies,

your body remembers,
hoards its wounds like a black hole,

your right wrist, thicker than your left,
that knobby protrusion
a talisman you rub,

while the blame feeds on itself.

Even now you know his death
was your fault.

Even now your body
yearns for him,

the arthritic ache that pulses an
image of his face,

a supernova, each time it rains.

My Dead Boy's Right Arm

My dead boy is at Staples Center,
a forward for the Lakers
in the last quarter
lightning fast, that trademark
cross-over dribble
down the court, passing to Kobe
who passes to Magic
who flicks it back to Josh who
saves the game in overtime with
a bank shot from heaven.

That's how I want to
remember him, on the court
where he was happiest.
Even after the amputation to save
his life, even after the cancer
hit him again, full-court press,
he remained firmly planted
in the game, even with
such a big chunk
of him gone.

It's almost night, the sky an
incandescent Laker purple
that always gives me hope
my boy's standing on the
far side of the court,
ready to run to me, hug me

with both arms, tell me,
"Mama, really, it's not so bad
being dead at 26."

God as Ice Cream Vendor

I took my heartache to Venice Beach, laid it out beside me on the sand, loaned it my spare beach towel and your green visor hat. Exhausted, I slept, but my heartache would not; it kept vigil in the August heat, one finger on my grief like an EMT. If you were here, we'd go for a swim, cruise the Boardwalk, lunch at the Sidewalk Cafe. But my heartache wouldn't hear of it. It wanted me to stay put. I craved an epiphany, God to reach down from the halcyon blue, and set me upright with you firmly planted beside me. So this time cancer could not knock you down. That day at the beach when you were little, I gave you a twenty for ice cream and you returned with no change. We marched into the store together and shamed the thief behind the counter, till he begged, "Just please don't call the cops!" You, my sweetness, licked the Rocky Road. "Stealing from a child?" I yelled across the freezer. "You're a real class act." I snatched back the twenty, like I wish I could snatch back your life.

It Rained Today in DTLA

—for Joshua, on the anniversary of his death

"It's a good thing you blew all that money your grandma
left you," I tell my son. We are driving home from yet
another round of chemo. We both know he is dying.
"Yeah, Mom," Josh smiles. "We had a fuckin' blast."

* * *

Hard September rain.
Maybe the first time weather
has mirrored my heart.

When You Think You're Ready to Pack Up Your Grief

Begin with his letterman's jacket.
Bundle it together with regret.

Stack sorrow on top of his class ring,
interspersed with his hip-hop CDs.

Loneliness should not be smoothed over the heart,
nor his childhood drawings folded in on themselves.

Don't tuck his senior portrait in the side pocket.

Lay it beside delicate items,
like feelings, face down;
place tissue paper on top.

Use additional layers to fold the last of him
in reverie, so it is engulfed.

Use this approach for your own heartbreak.

When friends ask to help, don't
spread the grief around. Keep it for yourself.
When the suitcase won't close, don't sit on it.
Don't even try to shut it.

when her son is dead seven years

1.
a woman is dancing on the moon,
a barefoot adagio of lilting beams.
she didn't know the light was so addictive.
her feet are cooking.
her arms are empty.

she thinks there is someone to feed.

2.
a woman is dancing on a cake plate
in her kitchen.
call her angel food. she skirts the frosting's edge,
skates straight to the bone-white middle.

she has a persistent memory.
she has a penchant for truth.
she has a life that is slipping away.

3.
a woman is skating barefoot on her sorrow,
her brain awash in the smell of his skin,
her arms shackled to the stars, a
pirouette of unmet promises,
regret. if she blames it on herself
she can fix it.

4.
a woman is taking her dead boy's eyes
to the moon.
she wants to show him the whole earth
before he finally gets some sleep.

5.
a woman is sleepwalking on the moon,
stardust clinging to her heels.
she's carrying life inside her
a luminescent, big-bellied Madonna.

she once loved a Russian poem
about a pregnant girl, chasing the moon;
but now she's forgotten who wrote it
and how the poem ends.
she just keeps chasing the moon.

and the moon, with *her* big belly, complicit,
out in the darkness, lighting the way.

End Notes

About the Author

Alexis Rhone Fancher's poems have appeared in numerous journals and literary magazines, including *Rattle, The MacGuffin, Slipstream, Chiron Review, Broad!, H_NGM_N, Fjords Review, Menacing Hedge, The Good Men Project, rawboned, Cactus Heart, Ragazine, Carbon Culture Review, Bare Hands Poetry, Blotterature, HOBART, Quaint Magazine, KYSO Flash, great weather for MEDIA, Serving House Journal, BLOOM, The Mas Tequila Review,* and elsewhere.

She has been published in over twenty anthologies and chapbooks, both in the U.S. and abroad. Her photographs have been published worldwide. Alexis is photography editor of *Fine Linen Literary Journal,* and poetry editor of *Cultural Weekly,* where she also publishes *The Poet's Eye*, a monthly photo essay about Los Angeles. She is the author of *How I Lost My Virginity to Michael Cohen: and other heart-stab poems* (Sybaritic Press, 2014).

Alexis is a member of Jack Grapes' L.A. Poets and Writers Collective. Since 2013 her work has been nominated for three Pushcart Prizes and four Best of The Net awards.

She and her husband Fancher live and collaborate in an eighth-floor loft/studio space in downtown Los Angeles. They have a spectacular view.

Photo Credits

With the exception of the portrait of mother and child on page 32, all photographs in this book are by the author.

p. 22   Rain, Downtown Los Angeles (DTLA, 2014)

p. 28   Black Raven, Blue Day (Marina del Rey, 2008)

p. 32   Joshua and Alexis (by Eric Rhone, 1981)

p. 38   I-10 Freeway South, Just Before DTLA (2013)

p. 40   It Rained Today in DTLA (September, 2015)

p. 42   a woman is dancing on the moon (photo collage, in collaboration with James Fancher, 2015)

p. 46   Window View (DTLA, 2014)

p. 51   Joshua Dorian Rhone (Marina del Rey, 2006)

Back Cover   Self-Portrait (Marina del Rey, 2007)

.

CPSIA information can be obtained
at www.ICGtesting.com
Printed in the USA
BVHW050341300519
549391BV00001B/2/P

* 9 7 8 0 9 8 6 2 7 0 3 2 1 *